PROMPT ME
HORROR & THRILLER

Creative Writing Workbook & Journal

Prompt Me Series

By
Robin Woods

Epic Books Publishing

A boutique publishing company

Lead Editor: Beth Braithwaite
Additional Editing: Brooke E. Wayne

All rights reserved. No part of this book may be reproduced or transmitted in any form or means, electronic or physical copies without permission in writing from the publisher or author. You can write to info@RobinWoodsFiction.com

Copyright © 2019 Robin Woods
First Edition

Cover Design created on Canva by Robin Woods

All Photos taken by Robin Woods

Thank you Beth, Glenn, and Tim for modeling for me.

All clip art taken from public domain sources.

Fonts: Century, Edo, and Calibri

Summary: A wide variety of writing prompts for maximum inspiration.

[Creative Writing, Diary, Non-Fiction, Reference, Writing Workbook, Fiction Writing, Writing Journal]

ISBN-10: 1-941077-18-8
ISBN-13: 978-1-941077-18-4

For a FREE Book and access to The Writer's Tool Kit, join the mailing list.

www.RobinWoodsFiction.com

TABLE OF CONTENTS

INTRODUCTION 7
    HOW TO USE THIS BOOK 7
PICTURE PROMPTS 9
STORY STARTERS   FIRST PERSON 45
    FIRST PERSON 47
STORY STARTERS   THIRD PERSON 57
    THIRD PERSON 59
USE THESE PHRASES 67
CHOOSE A PATH 75
DIALOGUE PROMPTS 83
    MORE DIALOGUE PROMPTS 93
FILL IN THE BLANK   49 POSSIBILITIES 95
GENERATE IT 101
    NAME YOUR THRILLER 103
    WHAT'S YOUR NIGHTMARE? 105
    WHO DUNNIT? 107
THAT'S CLASSIC 109
    CLASSIC CHARACTERS 111
    STOCK IT UP 113
    MAKE IT CREEPY 115
TRADITIONAL PROMPTS 117
    REMOVE A SENSE 119
    IF YOU WERE 121
    CHOOSE THE TRAITS 123
    MIXED BAG 125
    SELF DISCOVERY GONE WRONG 127
HAIKU 133
JOURNAL 137

REFERENCE 149
    DESCRIPTIVE ADJECTIVES 151
    SUPERSTITIONS 153
    CHARACTER MOTIVATIONS 154
    COMMON HORROR TROPES 155
    WORDS FOR SOUNDS 156
    CHARACTER NAMES 157
    CHARACTER APPEARANCE CHARTS 158
    HORROR VERSUS THRILLER 159
    CRIME & DETECTIVE VOCABULARY 160
    SYNONYMS 162
BOOKS BY ROBIN WOODS 168

INTRODUCTION

Writing is often messy, and sometimes we need a little help starting the process. When you begin to form your ideas, don't worry about grammar and punctuation. Simply writing the words down and experimenting are the most important parts. In order to become a better writer, you need to do three things:

1. Write often.
2. Read often.
3. Don't be afraid to make mistakes.

Embrace the mess, find your voice, and don't get discouraged.

> "You can always edit a bad page. You can't edit a blank page."
> — Jodi Picoult

Think of these pages as your artist's studio. Experiment with color and style. You never know; you may start something that grows into a masterpiece.

HOW TO USE THIS BOOK

This workbook is filled with a variety of different styles of prompts to help you decide what works best for you. If one style or prompt doesn't work, move on. If it doesn't work for you today, it might tomorrow.

If the pronouns don't work for you, change the she to a he, or vice versa. Prompts are meant to be inspiration, not shackles.

Carry it around with you. Mess it up. Use different kinds of ink. Stick Post-Its all over it.

Now, go forth and write!

PICTURE PROMPTS

It has often been said that a picture is worth a thousand words—but that doesn't really help writers. However, a picture can inspire thousands of words.

Use the following photos to create a unique story.

WRITING CHALLENGE:

Use at least three of the five senses in each of your stories—or add an extra sense.

☐ Sight ☐ Taste ☐ Touch ☐ Smell ☐ Sound

There are charts in the reference section in the back.

Picture Prompt How To

We are visual beings, so let's use our graphic nature to find inspiration. Following this page, you will find fifteen photo prompts. Use each of them as a muse for a story. It can be super short or the beginnings of a novel. This is a sample of what to do. When I see this picture, it reminds me of the waking with something in my room. So, here is my story:

Motion caused me to stir from my dream. A dark object kept blotting out the setting sun from my window. *I knew I'd regret the late nap.* Something deep within myself cautioned me from moving. As slow as possible, I opened my eyes to slits. What I'd thought was outside my room was actually inside of it.

The smell of gasoline and ancient body odor stung my nostrils. Pacing back and forth without sound was something bird-like and horrible. He, or maybe it, didn't seem to touch the floor, though when its back was turned, I saw oily tracks on my pale blue carpet.

Needing to know how much danger I was facing, I stirred like I was deep in sleep to see how it would react. Before I could shift my body an inch, it melted against the wall and became nothing more than a shadow. *Had it been in my head?* But the nauseating smell of body odor hadn't abated.

Stirring a second time, I rolled on my side towards the shadow and found that the shadow-bird wasn't the only thing in my bedroom. A gargantuan man in biker leathers sat in my wingback chair in the corner. He was chawing on what looked like an unlit cigar as he stared at me with intensity, but it was hard to tell due to only my eyes open a sliver. The shadow-bird moved above his head in a slow dance.

"Me pets been watching you." He chuckled, "I know you're awake. You kin stop pretendin'."

In one motion, I opened my eyes, sat up, and swung my legs to the floor as if my body was on a swivel. I exhaled a long, deep breath to keep myself calm and gather information. After a lengthy pause I asked, "Why have they been watching me?"

"You got no family and friends to speak of. No one would barely miss you."

"Well, you obviously haven't been watching me for long. I have lots of people who would miss me."

Something caressed my hair from behind. "They said you got spunk and a tongue for lies You'll love the underworld." Then the shadow-bird on the wall rushed at me, and darkness swallowed me.

1. TITLE: _____

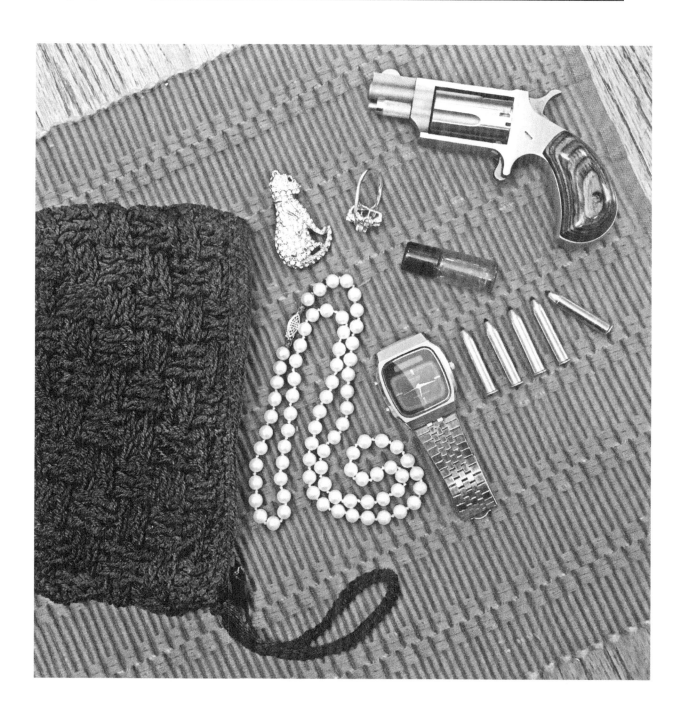

2. TITLE: _____

3. TITLE: _____

4. TITLE: _____

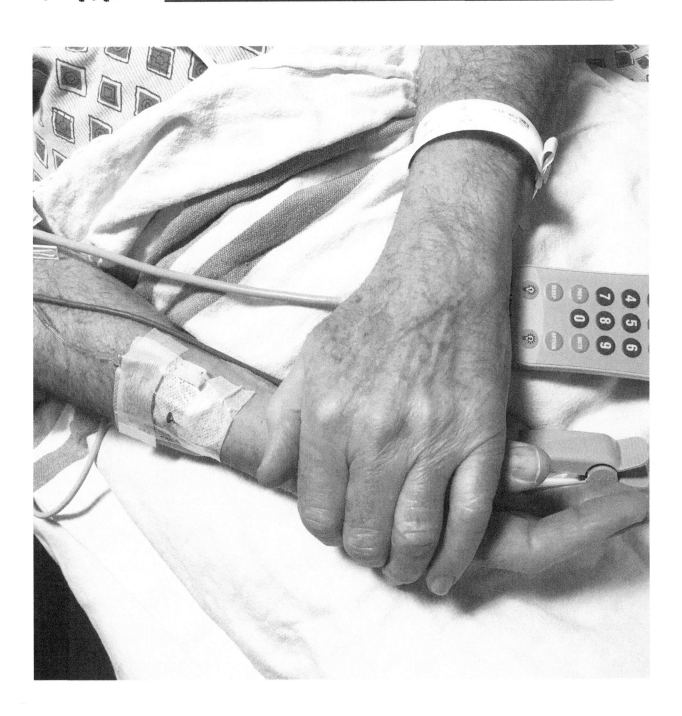

5. TITLE: _____

6. TITLE: _____

7. TITLE: _____

8. TITLE: _____

9. TITLE: _____

10. TITLE: _____

11. TITLE: _____

12. TITLE: _____

13. TITLE: _____

14. TITLE: _____

15. TITLE: _____

STORY STARTERS FIRST PERSON

Emotional Standpoint: Subjective
View: Limited
Pronoun Usage: I/we/us/me/my/mine/our/ours

WRITING CHALLENGE:

Limit the amount of times your character "felt" or "feels" something. Use active voice to help keep the reader in the experience.

FIRST PERSON

16. Hiding in a room filled with pointy objects was the last place they'd check for me.
17. When smoke curled around his head, I prayed that he was smoking a cigarette. But I feared that I wasn't that lucky…
18. I'd been told with perfect clarity to never push the button. So, I pushed it.
19. His passive-aggressive behavior was slowly breaking me down. I could see exactly what he was doing, but I felt powerless to defend myself against his crazy.
20. Reaching my go bag was priority one. Now, I only had to get past six armed men.
21. Legends about this stretch of the woods scared the bravest of men, but I was much too stupid to be frightened.
22. Our "game" was turning into a deranged version of tag. But this one left dead bodies…
23. Going for a walk in the woods late at night seemed really cliché, but I wasn't sure what else I could do. I was out of food, water, and fuel. And daylight was when…
24. Paint fumes assaulted my senses. *Why had they painted again so soon?* I went…
25. *Scratch, scratch, scratch* invaded my consciousness, but it wasn't the tree branch on my window this time…
26. When we passed the pet cemetery, I shuddered. The film had ruined…
27. The sharpening of knives was all I could hear. It was a sound I'd grown up hearing every time my father used the kitchen, but now…
28. Clank. Drag. Clank. Drag. Clank. I braced myself for what was about to emerge…
29. The TOP SECRET stamp glared at me for a whole two seconds before I ripped the folder open. Two seconds after that, I knew it was the-worst-decision-ever…
30. All I had to do was make a wish, but I wondered about the consequence…
31. Through the blindfold, I gathered as much information as possible. It smelled like rusty metal, bleach, and cilantro. I wasn't sure which had me more worried.
32. With a snap she opened the map, revealing our next challenge…
33. Blinking slowly, I wondered if they were supposed to have wings. My grin widened; *they were so beautiful.* Yet at the same time, I wondered why fear was wriggling…
34. I liked the melodic sound of his voice, and I followed it even when he…

35. It returned to my head again like an incessant drum urging me to...
36. We'd been warned to not ignore our history. I guess the authorities shouldn't have burned all of our books; they wouldn't forget this blast from the past.
37. I begged myself not to walk down the dark hall, but then I did anyway...
38. A ripple running beneath the underbrush had me hoisting myself onto the nearest tree branch. *Better safe than sorry*. But, the moment...
39. This was an escape room created by a lunatic. *I guess I should get myself into therapy.*
40. The old crone had warned me about this exact situation. If only I'd written down her directions.
41. Swinging open the door, I was faced with a room full of dolls.
42. My fingers grazed something unfamiliar in my pocket. I pulled out a note that said, "I have her now. And you have nothing."
43. His black eyes raked over me, but his stony expression showed nothing...
44. "What does 'Slay the Day' mean anyway? *Am I Santa Claus or a serial killer?*" I grumbled my way down the hall, but then it struck me...
45. "What is your problem?" I hollered, but realized that was a mistake...
46. *I thought all car trunks were supposed to have release levers now.* I pricked my fingers as I felt around again, but...
47. I watched as the shadows between the buildings in the distance seemed to converge...
48. My Grandpa always told me not to go into the basement after midnight. *What did he know anyway?*
49. She paced back and forth, her mask more menacing now that I couldn't ...
50. I knew talking out loud wasn't going to make me any safer, but it almost made me feel like I wasn't alone in the creepy woods without a flashlight or cell signal...
51. My opinion was that the legends of vampires and werewolves had to be fake...
52. I tried to shuffle slowly to keep the glass from cutting my bare feet—and not to make noise...
53. For a long moment, I wondered if I was dead, but decided it was...
54. He was misreading my every thought and gesture. It was like he'd memorized the "How to be Creepy Guidebook." But maybe it wasn't just an act...
55. It worried me. Something about the windows in the old house didn't look right...

56. Old slasher films had nothing on this guy—he was a new breed of…
57. Being locked in the back of a truck with a mouth breather was the least of my worries. If I didn't call my service with a code by midnight, the reapers would be released…
58. Something about me was scaring people away…
59. If only cats really did have a "murder button." I'd push that button and huck that cat across the room to destroy them this minute…
60. All of it had been a carefully executed web of lies dating back a century. And now…
61. Every new moon we could hear laughter of children coming from the forest, but the night scope cameras never picked up a whisper of movement…
62. It started as a low moan, then a gurgle. Then, everything went black…
63. I wondered how I could possibly end up at a carnival after hours, on a full moon, and with a car that won't start. But then, I realized it's me. Of course I'm here.
64. As I woke, I realized my hands were shackled to my sides. *What had they done to me?*
65. The unearthly howl of wolves and the scuttle of unusually large feet pattered ever closer. I didn't have long before…
66. Over and over, I tried to open my eyes, but they were glued shut—literally.
67. I gulped a breath. Then said, "The last time I saw you, they were covering your grave, and I was dragged into the woods trying to scream my way back to you."
68. The gooey sounds were much more disturbing than I thought they'd be…
69. When the police flipped a quick U-turn and idled up behind me, I knew the situation was about to escalate. If they only…
70. The house phone rang, and when I answered, it went dead—like it had been cut.
71. He told me if I refused to obey, spoke my mind, or challenged him again, he'd have me charged with witchcraft. But, instead of…
72. Saving the world wasn't going to be easy, but I had a plan to…
73. A glint of light made his eyes look red for a fraction of a second. *Or was it not a trick of the light?* I swallowed hard and stumbled back a step.
74. After dragging my hand through my hair, I found it full of tiny insects that…
75. Suppressing an eye roll, I yelled out, "If you are trying to scare me, ghosts are so last year." Then something stroked my arm from behind…

PROMPT # ____ YOUR TITLE: _____

PROMPT # ____ YOUR TITLE: _____

PROMPT # ____ YOUR TITLE: _____

PROMPT # ___ YOUR TITLE: _____

PROMPT # ____ YOUR TITLE: _____

PROMPT # ___ YOUR TITLE: _____

PROMPT # ____ YOUR TITLE: _____

STORY STARTERS THIRD PERSON

Third Person Limited
Emotional Standpoint: Objective
View: Limited
Pronoun Usage: he/she/it/him/his/her/they/their

Third Person Omniscient
Emotional Standpoint: Objective
View: Unlimited
Pronoun Usage: he/she/it/him/his/her/they/their

Deep Third Person
Emotional Standpoint: Subjective
View: Limited
Pronoun Usage: he/she/it/him/his/her/they/their

WRITING CHALLENGE:

Vary your language, especially your sentence openings. I.e. Not every sentence should begin with "The" or "Then."

THIRD PERSON

76. The skeletal trees looked like broken teeth in a gaping mouth...
77. He groaned to himself, "Just follow the screams and you'll find them. Nothing to worry about at all." Without any other hesitation, he set off to...
78. Light, glittering laughter chimed through the crowd until a booming...
79. She debated whether to stand her ground or flee. Her heart wanted to stay, but her feet were saying...
80. Each of them were linked in their dreams, but had no idea that...
81. His grin faded to seriousness. "If they say the words, I won't be able to stop." Then he clutched the knife in his hand until his knuckles turned white.
82. Sweeping the powdery sand from her bruised legs, she...
83. With shaking hands, he loosed the card from the envelope to reveal a real "Get Out of Jail Free" card. *Careful consideration would...*
84. A fresh coat of paint and a lot of bleach should fix the problem, but...
85. For the third night in a row, she woke from a deep sleep with muddy feet and dead grass in her sheets. But this time, she'd set up a camera...
86. After collecting dust for years, something inside the safe began to stir...
87. He backed away from the window in two fluid strides as the blood drained from his face. "I'm pretty sure I just saw my first grade teacher. She died ten years ago."
88. Congestion clogged the intersection, leaving her no choice but to...
89. For a long time the scratching sound under the floor was small, like a rat had found its way inside. Then it became loud and the floorboards groaned...
90. Scratching his head in confusion, he asked, "How can you be so nice and so evil at once?"
91. For days she didn't speak, and when she did, it silenced everyone. "Normal people scare me. They are too breakable."
92. Harvesting herbs from the garden was part of his morning ritual, but today...
93. Getting through a room full of imposters without setting off an alarm was the least of his problems. It was the fact that his partner was now...
94. She was not in the mood to hunt monsters today—the last one had ruined her shoes.
95. He wondered how smart it was to follow the gypsy's advice; it seemed sound...

96. Her first step in saving the world was not to die in this situation…
97. The bloodroot plant, *Sanguinaria Canadensis*, was so deceptively pretty he mused. Happy white flowers that cause vomiting and organ failure, perfect for…
98. Blinking rapidly, she stared at the words "Game Over," refusing to…
99. After months of digging at the archeological site, he found the hidden room he'd been searching for—and it was undisturbed. But when he crossed the threshold…
100. Being on the run was routine. A simple series of rules that had to be followed, but when she rounded the corner…
101. Proving herself was going to take more than words…
102. Scorn colored his tone. "I don't get scared—ever." Then he flung the door wide and stepped into the darkness…
103. When she woke, a scorpion was casually strolling down her shin towards her foot…
104. According to Sherlock, "Once you eliminate the impossible, whatever remains, no matter how improbable, must be the truth." But he couldn't accept…
105. It blinked and cocked its head at an inhuman angle before lunging…
106. The meal was an exquisite blend of savory ingredients that enraptured her, each bite more delicious than the last. By the time she was finished, she hadn't noticed…
107. Some punk in a mask and hoodie wasn't going to stop…
108. Packages started arriving with things he hadn't actually ordered. All he'd done was mutter under his breath that he needed more toilet paper or shampoo. Not long after…
109. Annoyed, she trotted past the ghost of yet another person her mother had killed…
110. He hesitated for a long moment before speaking. "Just because you're my sister doesn't mean I can favor you. The house always wins."
111. Every bird chirping, "Good morning," fell silent at the same second…
112. She was unaware that the amulet she'd been given for protection, was stealing a day of her life as payment, for each day it shielded her.
113. Screech, clomp, screech, clomp….
114. Even the darkest shadows stilled when she drew near. The dirt itself, afraid to crunch under her feet.
115. Bending over like a ragdoll, she tried to release the tension in her lower back. It had been a long time since she'd had to fight like that. It felt good…

116. First, the fire leapt to the drapes in a beautiful arc before…
117. Bells clamored above the city that was smothered by unrelenting fog so thick it seemed impenetrable.
118. He was determined to be good. He couldn't go back to jail again; it would…
119. Unable to take it any longer, she tossed the doll in the dumpster in the alley. Its eyes were too real and seemed to follow her. But when she woke the next day, it was…
120. Sunset was at 8:43 PM. They didn't have long…
121. She felt a pinch on her scalp and realized that the woman in green had cut a lock of her hair as she'd passed and was slipping it into a satin pouch.
122. "No Trespassing" seemed to be an invitation to the loners and rebels of the area…
123. Ranting was the only word he could use to describe the voice in his head. But what it was telling him to do would put him in danger…
124. Tomorrow the super blood moon would peak at 3:00 AM. Everyone with…
125. Black capes and leather pants were a little cliché, but it seemed to create a mood that blue jeans and a t-shirt couldn't capture…
126. In the churning clouds above, they could see mammoth, winged creatures in the…
127. The abrupt bleat of his alarm woke him immediately—something was wrong. When he tried the bedroom door, it was screwed shut. *How hadn't he heard it?*
128. He thought the abandoned prison would be the ultimate place to hide, but…
129. Sarah had always dreamt she had a twin. It had felt so real, and when her parents passed, she found pictures proving it was true. *Why had they hidden it from her?*
130. Frowning, he replied to the air, "Imaginary friends aren't supposed to talk back."
131. Dust filtered from the top of the building, drawing her attention, seconds before the gargoyle sprang to life…
132. *Stealing werewolf pups from their parents probably wasn't ideal*, she thought.
133. He had two choices—reveal that he wasn't human and had been feeding off of them in their sleep, or leave with the harvesters and be tried for treason…
134. Something moved under his skin at the base of his tattoo…
135. Scientists built a machine to tear open the veil between worlds, but the plans had been sent from the other side. The scientists hadn't considered why they'd received the plans…

PROMPT # ____ YOUR TITLE: _____

PROMPT # ____ YOUR TITLE: _____

PROMPT # ____ YOUR TITLE: _____

PROMPT # ____ YOUR TITLE: _____

PROMPT # ____ YOUR TITLE: _____

USE THESE PHRASES

WRITING CHALLENGE:

Writers often forget to incorporate the sense of smell into their writings. Try to use this sense in an offbeat way. An inspirational chart is in the back.

136. Choose and use at least six of these ten phrases:

cacophony of cries	overwhelming scent of roses
liquid movement	puckering from the sour taste
thick with oily residue	the scuffling of shoes
burble of running water	an acute, burning sensation
ominous, black shape	with a tight expression

137. Choose and use at least seven of these ten phrases:

damp chilled his very bones	burst of citrus fruit
smooth feel of silk	warm like melted butter
ethereal sound of laughing children	guttural sound spewed
clanking of yard tools	groaning to life
fog curled and weaved through branches	dappled sunlight filtered

138. Choose and use at least eight of these ten phrases:

inviting aroma of slow-cooked stew	throaty chuckle
slumped in defeat	eye-crinkling smile
howl of contempt	enraptured with joy
weighted with humidity	scratch of coarse wool
swish of long skirts	groped through the darkness

139. Choose and use at least nine of these ten phrases:

bellowing train whistle	with wicked delight
malevolent grin	gritty dirt under her nails
enthusiasm of a ten-year-old	moon-drenched skies
tasted like garlic and despair	lumbering past houses
scent of polished wood	shimmering with ice and danger

140. Choose and use at least nine of these ten phrases:

lazy spire of smoke	odor of rotting leaves
scampered sideways evading	mystified the crowd
hands red with blood	she seemed to shrivel
seized him roughly	cried out into the abyss
gong of the bell tower	felt the slime of the mossy steps

141. Choose and use at least nine of these ten phrases:

moon, shrouded in darkness	shuffled woodenly
crush of an angry crowd	feet scraping the ground
smell of ash and soot	flutter of silk
comfort of steaming tea	smooth, glossy marble
swirl of dust in the air	door snicked shut

CHOOSE A PATH

WRITING CHALLENGE:

Use at least three of the five senses in each of your stories.

☐ Sight ☐ Sound ☐ Hearing ☐ Taste ☐ Touch

If your story has fantasy elements, you can always add a sixth sense.

142. **Skidding to a stop in the forest,...**
- ☐ she swerved into a turnout and headed back to the city.
- ☐ he realized he was being followed.
- ☐ she was face-to-face with the man in the mask.
- ☐ he listened for a moment, then he heard the howl.
- ☐ she decided to stop running and start fighting—dirty.

143. **The old cemetery at the end of the street was...**
- ☐ the meeting spot for all the ghosts in the northern hemisphere.
- ☐ experiencing earthquakes in the darkest hours of the night.
- ☐ his hiding spot whenever the nightmares had gotten bad.
- ☐ filled with more flowers than a florist shop.
- ☐ being moved for a new strip mall.

144. **Horrible light pulsed from…**
- ☐ the bottom of the bubbling swamp.
- ☐ the airship floating over the burning field.
- ☐ his fingertips before it became blinding.
- ☐ the churning machine that seemed to be alive.
- ☐ the basement, eerily in sync with her sprinting heart.

145. Kidnapping her was an accident...

- ☐ , but there was no going back.
- ☐ , or so the police thought—but they only had part of the story.
- ☐ waiting to happen. She was the worst.
- ☐ though, not really. He'd wanted to save her from her life for years.
- ☐ that would have been the best thing that had ever happened.

146. People were disappearing every night...

- ☐ , despite roaming security combing the streets.
- ☐ ; it was as if they were being beamed away.
- ☐ ; the government was out of control.
- ☐ into large board rooms and making secret plans.
- ☐ , since the smugglers were doing their job so well.

147. Ushering them down the staircase,…

- ☐ he made them shackle themselves into the cage.
- ☐ she swept her arm wide, revealing a veritable playground of tools.
- ☐ he chuckled at the irony of the situation.
- ☐ they couldn't believe it was
- ☐ she noticed the party decorations looked oddly real.

DIALOGUE PROMPTS

A few tips before we start:

- ☐ Avoid using the characters' names too much in dialogue.
- ☐ Make sure not all of your characters sound the same.
- ☐ Try not to have characters parrot or repeat the previous sentence.

WRITING CHALLENGE:

Use as few adverbs as possible.

- ☐ Generally, people don't speak in complete sentences. Use some fragments.
- ☐ Play with dialect and the way your characters use contractions.
- ☐ Restarts, stumbles, and stutters can improve emotional scenes.

148. "So, what's your master plan?"

"Survive. Then, eat chocolate. Lots of chocolate."

149. "I'm what monsters fear at night."

"Comforting. You realize you sound like a B list action star, right?"

150. "In the span of ten minutes you've broken a mirror, walked under a ladder, and spilled salt."

"Obviously, I'm trying to trigger the apocalypse."

151. "Meh. Murder…missing person. If they can't prove it, it's all semantics."

"But I didn't tell you who's missing."

152. "I decided to Google myself, but—"

"It led you to me. That was a terrible, terrible mistake."

153. "I'm completely exposed out here. Am I supposed to be the bait?"

"Pretty *and* smart. Who would've guessed? Now, get down."

154. "You know the nerd always survives these things, right?"

"Playing video games with your little brother once a month doesn't change your status as a jock, dude."

155. "I'm not dead now; that's all that matters."

"Wait, you didn't fake your death?"

MORE DIALOGUE PROMPTS...

156. "I'm going on a walk."

    "I'll come with you."

    "I don't need a babysitter."

    "Nah, if you get eaten by a bear, I need to take pictures for the insurance."

157. "You seem nervous."

    "It's all to lull you into my confidence so I can sell you."

158. "If you want my opinion—"

    "Ha, I don't. I can screw things up on my own without your help."

    "Okay, but it's about a detour to avoid that ambush."

159. "Once you bury it, it should stay dead."

    "Should? Did someone change the rules when I wasn't looking?"

160. "That bat just bit me."

    "Oh, my gosh, are you okay?"

    "I feel…oddly alive."

161. "You know he's corrupt, don't you?"

    "I do. I'm his assassin, and you know too much."

PROMPT # _____ **YOUR TITLE** _____

FILL IN THE BLANK 49 POSSIBILITIES

WRITING CHALLENGE:

Try writing from a different point of view. For added challenge, write the same scene twice, from two different perspectives.

162. When _____ the death of an old family friend, he/she finds that _____.

Blank One	Blank Three
researching	his death has triggered an ancient curse
stumbling across	it wasn't a heart attack like the authorities claimed
investigating	she was actually a Russian spy
discovering	something supernatural caused her death
faced with	he is now being followed by the men in black
reading about	the nightmares she's been having are true
mourning	he has ties to a powerful crime family

163. Night after night, _____ after the _____.

Blank One	Blank Two
trolls marched the streets	guards drifted to sleep
it looked like Halloween	sun sputtered and became erratic
she hid more money	rebels began to rise up
things slithered in the darkness	stars started to lose their light
he watched for a sign	clocks started running backwards
one was chosen to be bitten	humans had to go into hiding
the prisoners escaped	adults started disappearing

164. The house _____ was filled with

_____.

Blank One	Blank Two
of horrors	screams loud enough to be heard outside
in my old neighborhood	a mixture of mind-controlling medicinals
exploded and	memories and regrets
shifted and swayed and	dolls with the captures souls of people
in all of my nightmares	dusty scarecrows and aging mannequins
stood ominously and	smoldering creatures made of fire
brand of coffee	jack-in-the-box ghosts and plastic zombies

GENERATE IT

WRITING CHALLENGE:

Give your character a secret that influences all of his or her decisions.

NAME YOUR THRILLER

165. Use the generator to create a title, and then write a fitting story for the title.

THRILLER GENERATOR

THE _____ _____

First Letter of First Name
- A. Ancient
- B. Broken
- C. Cunning
- D. Dead
- E. Eigth
- F. First
- G. Grey
- H. Hostile
- I. Iron
- J. Justified
- K. Killing
- L. Lost
- M. Mortal
- N. Necessary
- O. Obscure
- P. Painted
- Q. Quiet
- R. Ruined
- S. Steel
- T. Tenth
- U. Unfortunate
- V. Vacant
- W. Winter
- X. Xanthous*
- Y. Yellow
- Z. Zenith's

*Xanthous--greenish orange

First Letter of Last Name
- A. Station
- B. City
- C. Block
- D. Door
- E. Fareway
- F. Embassy
- G. Gateway
- H. Informant
- I. Highway
- J. Jealousy
- K. Lane
- L. Kiss
- M. Directive
- N. Nemesis
- O. Player
- P. Oasis
- Q. Revelation
- R. Queen
- S. Trap
- T. Street
- U. Fire
- V. Villa
- W. Yield
- X. Prayer
- Y. Zodiac
- Z. Widow

What's Your Nightmare?

166. Use the generator to create a nightmare to fuel your story.

Nightmare Generator

1. First Letter of Your Last Name

- A. Angry
- B. Burly
- C. Cadaverous
- D. Desperate
- E. Evil
- F. Phantom
- G. Giant
- H. Hellish
- I. Irritating
- J. Jinxed
- K. Killer
- L. Lonely
- M. Malevolent
- N. Nimble
- O. Oily
- P. Putrid
- Q. Quick
- R. Robotic
- S. Spawning
- T. Terrible
- U. Urban
- V. Vicious
- W. Withered
- X. Xiphoidic (swordlike)
- Y. Yucky
- Z. Zealous

2. Last Digit of Your Birth Date

0. Spiders
1. Aliens
2. Clowns
3. Psycho Killers
4. Cannibals
5. Snakes
6. Vampires
7. Ghosts
8. Scorpions
9. Undead

3. Last Digit of Your Birth Year

0. In the Boathouse
1. Under the Bed
2. In the Basement
3. In the Emergency Room
4. At Midnight
5. In an Abandoned Zoo
6. In a Dark Alley
7. On the Lake
8. In the Woods
9. In the Saw Mill

Alternate:
1. First Letter of Your First Name
2. Last Digit of Your Address
3. Last Digit of Your Phone Number

WHO DUNNIT?

167. Your character just died. Use the cause of death to create a story.

CAUSE OF DEATH

The official cause of death was _____, but what really happened was you were _____ by (a/an) _____.

OFFICIAL CAUSE
Last Digit of Your Address

0. heart attack
1. car accident
2. falling downstairs
3. died in sleep
4. food poisoning
5. brain aneurysm
6. old age
7. appendicitis
8. pneumonia
9. plane crash

REAL CAUSE
Last Digit of Your Zip Code

0. choked
1. sliced
2. drowned
3. strangled
4. stabbed
5. infected
6. impaled
7. poisoned
8. crushed
9. smothered

WEAPON USED
First Letter of Your Name

A. murder of crows
B. army of drones
C. box of clown shoes
D. nuclear waste
E. zombie police officer
F. jagged toenail
G. escaped convict
H. gaggle of geese
I. rusty shovel
J. evil icicles
K. bag of rocks
L. circus elephant
M. sack of potatoes
N. Samari sword
O. rusty paperclips
P. meteorite
Q. slithering rattlesnakes
R. renegade robots
S. gremlins
T. crispy tofu
U. flaming spear
V. cursed arrow
W. mutant spider
X. undead German Shepherd
Y. broken garden shears
Z. giant octopus tentacle

THAT'S CLASSIC

WRITING CHALLENGE:

Have one of your characters be ruled by superstitions. A chart is in the back to help.

CLASSIC CHARACTERS

Use these famous characters to inspire a totally different story. Don't worry—all of these characters are in the public domain. There are no limits on the use of them. Woot!

168. Abraham Van Helsing
169. The Black Knight
170. Captain Nemo
171. The Creature from the Black Lagoon
172. Dr. Jekyll
173. Dorian Gray
174. Dracula
175. Faust
176. Frankenstein's Monster
177. The Grim Reaper
178. Hamlet
179. The Headless Horseman
180. The Hunchback of Notre Dame
181. James Moriarty
182. Jack the Ripper
183. King Kong
184. Lady Serpent
185. The Lock Ness Monster
186. Moby Dick
187. The Mummy
188. Mystico
189. The Phantom of the Opera
190. The Queen of Hearts
191. Red Riding Hood
192. Rumpelstiltskin
193. Sweeney Todd
194. The Time Traveler
195. Wilhelmina Murray
196. The Wolf Man

PROMPT # ___ YOUR TITLE: _____

STOCK IT UP

Mixing and matching stock characters is a great way to start working with your cast. These classics are ripe for the horror and thriller genres. Write a series of stories combining two or more characters into one.

197. Aloof, Dark-Haired Girl
198. Byronic Hero
199. Creepy Housekeeper
200. Damsel in Distress
201. Doppelgänger
202. The Do-Gooder
203. Decrepit Caretaker
204. Eerie, Pale-Skinned Brunette
205. Evil Mentor
206. Evil Prince
207. Evil Twin
208. Evil Sorcerer
209. Femme Fatale
210. The Highwayman
211. Hunter of Monsters
212. Demon Slayer
213. The Igor
214. The Incorruptible One
215. The Ingénue
216. Jack the Ripper
217. Jekyll & Hyde
218. Lady in Red
219. Mad Scientist
220. Madwoman in the Attic
221. Naïve Newcomer
222. Poisonous Friend
223. Seer
224. Serial Killer
225. The Sociopath
226. Stalker
227. The Vamp
228. The Virgin
229. Wicked Witch
230. Woman Scorned

Add a Classic Setting

Abandoned Lodge
Always Day
Always Night
Ancient Tomb
Bell Tower
Boarding School
Creepy Cathedral
Creepy Cemetery
Criminal Convention
The Grand Ball
Impending Disaster
Interrogation Chamber
Forbidden Forest
Foreign Embassy
Evil Tower
The Institute
Ghost Ship
Ghost Train
Haunted Castle
Haunted House
Room 101
Secluded Town
Secret Bunker
Secret Room
Serial Killer Convention
Spy Convention
Mad Scientist Laboratory
The House is Alive
Town with a Dark Secret
The Mysterious Invitation
The Thirteen Floor

PROMPT # ___ YOUR TITLE: _____

MAKE IT CREEPY

Anything can be made creepy if you do it right. Here's a list of common items. Your task is to turn each everyday item into a story. Maybe, the shoes actually belonged to Hitler (that cause the wearer to do terrible things) or a hair comb that belonged to Marie Antoinette (that brings spirits from the past to the present). The possibilities are limitless.

231. Dinner Plate
232. Railroad Tracks
233. Cowboy Boots
234. TV Remote
235. Pearl Necklace
236. Hair Brush
237. Oil Lamp
238. Stained Glass
239. Wine Goblet
240. Hammer
241. Pocket Knife
242. Oil-painted Portrait
243. Copper Pot
244. Keys
245. Silver Earrings
246. Worry Stone
247. Hand Mirror
248. Compass
249. Reading Glasses
250. Vase
251. Arrowhead
252. Lighter
253. Feather Pen
254. Wedding Dress
255. Serving Fork

PROMPT # ____ YOUR TITLE: _____

TRADITIONAL PROMPTS

WRITING CHALLENGE:

Add sound to your story. A chart of words for sounds is in the back.

REMOVE A SENSE

256. Your character can't <u>smell</u> and the bottom floor of his building is on fire. The fire alarms aren't working.

257. Your character can't <u>hear</u> and there's a blackout. Something inhuman infiltrates the city.

258. Chose a sense to dampen. How does it impact your character?

PROMPT # _____ YOUR TITLE: _____

IF YOU WERE

If you were ___, who/what would you be? Or how would you act? Explain by telling a story, using vivid verbs and sensory images.

259. a lunatic

260. a counter-intelligence agent

261. a psychoanalyst

262. a foreign exchange student

263. a police inspector

264. a serial killer

265. a sniper

266. a criminal

267. a sentinel

268. a federal marshal

269. a corrupt politician

270. a kidnap victim

271. a CIA handler

272. a forensic scientist

273. a stalker

274. a family dog in the aftermath of a crime

Add a Complication

A. trapped across the border of a hostile country

B. locked in the basement of a stranger

C. the locks won't work in the car and something is outside

D. police hounds are hot on your trail

E. your arch nemesis is stuck in a public bathroom with you

F. airport security has pulled you into a room for questioning

G. convicted of a crime you didn't commit

H. shot with a tranquilizer dart while escaping

I. you find out your best friend is really a ghost

PROMPT # ___ YOUR TITLE: _____

CHOOSE THE TRAITS

275. Your character is a sociopath. Use the list below to inspire a story with a character who suffers from anti-social personality disorder.

SOCIOPATHS

- Nervous and easily agitated
- No impulse control
- Callousness
- Witty
- Habitual liar
- Unreliable
- Doesn't plan things
- Doesn't learn from mistakes
- Manipulative
- Narcissistic
- Superficial charm
- Needs lots of stimulation
- Shallow emotions
- Irresponsible
- Lack of loyalty
- Chameleon
- Juvenile delinquency
- Lack of remorse
- Grandiose sense of self
- No shame or guilt
- Cunning
- Deceitful
- Hostile
- Risky behavior
- No empathy
- Arrogance
- Abusive relationships
- Ignoring social norms
- Fired from jobs
- Physical fights
- Having few friends
- Intense eye contact
- Disregard for right and wrong
- Conning others for profit or pleasure
- Doesn't understand other people's emotions

PROMPT # ____ YOUR TITLE: _____

MIXED BAG

A little mix of everything to keep it interesting.

276. Little gifts start appearing on your character's desk at work, days later at the front doorstep, then inside the bedroom…

277. You are an assassin reaching retirement age and people don't want to hire you because of your age. To prove your worth, you hire the best younger assassin to kill you.

278. The Garden of Eden is discovered in a remote ravine, but the Tree of Knowledge of Good and Evil isn't what we thought it was.

279. Your character shuffles out to the kitchen to make morning coffee and finds a freshly brewed pot and Frankenstein's monster sitting at the table.

280. After being accused of ignoring friends in public places for years, you run face-to-face into the evil twin you didn't know you had.

281. When you look in the mirror, the whole thing goes black like the lights are off, but the bathroom is fully illuminated. Then it clears up, and the only thing black is your eyes.

282. You get your bank statement and find that money has been funneled to a different account. And what is paid for sends you into panic mode.

283. On a remote road, you pull over to eat at a café and find your exact car with the same license plate as yours parked in front.

284. Your grandfather passes away. In order to get the inheritance, you have to live in his house for a year—but it's haunted.

285. Using a new GPS app, it repeatedly tries to take you to a location you have never programmed in or been to. One day, you decide to go there.

286. For days, the creepy neighbor kid has been coming over and pointing at a date on the calendar saying, "Ruoy Larenuf." Then you realize it's "your funeral" backwards.

287. When you go into a gas station bathroom, a nervous girl scampers past you. After glancing out the door at her retreating figure, you find a note. "Please help me."

288. Your character works in a small convenience store. Every Thursday a customer comes in, circles the store, and leaves without buying anything. After two years of doing this, he comes to the counter with a small silver box and says, "This is the end of all of it."

PROMPT # ____ YOUR TITLE: _____

SELF DISCOVERY GONE WRONG

289. How are you the villain in your own story? Explain.

290. You have been given three million dollars, but you have to spend it in three days, and no one can know you've ever had the money. How do you spend it?

291. A comet makes a low pass through the earth's atmosphere. The next day you feel odd. Why? What is your plan of action? Are you alone?

292. You just killed someone on purpose. What drove you to do it?

293. Someone knowingly infected you with a hideous disease. What do you do? Map out a plan of action.

294. It's obvious blackmail is the answer. Who will you blackmail and why?

295. If you had to get out of town and stay off the grid, where would you go? How would you stay hidden?

296. You have to stay overnight in a haunted house. What is your plan?

297. The police try to arrest you, but they keep looking at each other with seditious grins. Do you trust them and go peaceably? Who do you call?

298. You have a dark secret that could get someone killed. What is it? Why are you keeping it a secret? What will happen if it gets out?

299. If people in your neighborhood started mulling about with expressionless faces ignoring you, what would you do?

300. You discover a treasure map from the 1800s in an abandoned bank's safe deposit box. There is a warning on the map. Do you ignore it or go for it? Explain.

301. If you had a superpower and could only use it for evil, what would it be and what would you do?

302. Your worst nightmare comes to life. What is it? How do you deal with it? How will you prevent it from happening again?

303. A helicopter lands on your street. The pilot motions for you to come to him. What do you do? Why? Note: There is a tiger wearing a headset in the co-pilot's seat.

PROMPT # ____ YOUR TITLE: _____

PROMPT # ____ YOUR TITLE: _____

PROMPT # _____ YOUR TITLE: _____

PROMPT # ____ YOUR TITLE: _____

PROMPT #_____ YOUR TITLE: _____

HAIKU
A PRACTICE IN BREVITY

WRITING CHALLENGE:

Tap into some diverse emotions: hope, happiness, sadness, indifference, and need. Then, write haikus from the perspective of different characters.

Haikus are a great way to practice precise language. They are three lines long. The first line is five syllables, the second is seven, and the third is five (5-7-5). Here are a few examples.

They can be about triumph:

> Conquering my fears 5
> my destiny is my own, 7
> I rise up with grace. 5
>
> —Robin Woods

Or hopeless:

> YOU THINK I AM TRAPPED. 5
> I SMILE TIGHTLY IN HATE, 7
> KNOWING I WILL LEAVE. 5
>
> —Robin Woods

Or a call to action:

> Make the world better. 5
> One small kindness at a time, 7
> Start with a smile. 5
>
> —Robin Woods

304. About love:

_____ 5

_____ 7

_____ 5

305. About loss:

_____ 5

_____ 7

_____ 5

306. About something evil:

_____ 5

_____ 7

_____ 5

307. About a character:

_____ 5

_____ 7

_____ 5

308. About your dreams:

_____ 5

_____ 7

_____ 5

309. About friendship:

_____ 5
_____ 7
_____ 5

310. About the city:

_____ 5
_____ 7
_____ 5

311. Your choice:

_____ 5
_____ 7
_____ 5

312. Your choice:

_____ 5
_____ 7
_____ 5

313. Your choice:

_____ 5
_____ 7
_____

JOURNAL

WRITING CHALLENGE:

Use this space as a traditional journal or for a list of story ideas that were inspired by the prompts.

REFERENCE

REFERENCE WITHIN THE WORKBOOK

List of Classic Characters..........................110
List of Stock Characters............................113
Nightmare Generator...............................105
Thriller Generator......................................103
Cause of Death...107
Sociopath Traits..123

MY WORD LISTS:

DESCRIPTIVE ADJECTIVES

	DESCRIPTIVE ADJECTIVES
A	Able, Abundant, Accepting, Accommodating, Active, Addictive, Adequate, Aggressive, Alive, Amazing, Amiable, Amicable, Amusing, Antagonistic, Anxious, Apathetic, Aquatic, Arrogant, Articulate, Artistic, Attentive, Attractive, Ashamed, Authoritative, Awesome
B	Barren, Benevolent, Bewildered, Biased, Biodegradable, Blasé, Blushing, Bold, Bonding, Boorish, Bountiful, Brainy, Braggart, Brave, Brilliant, Bright, Buoyant, Busy, Buzz
C	Callow, Calm, Captious, Caring, Celestial, Charming, Chaste, Cheat, Cheerful, Churlish, Civil, Clean, Clever, Clumsy, Coarse, Coastal, Cold, Colossal, Combative, Combustible, Comfortable, Commercial, Communicative, Compact, Competitive, Compulsive, Condemned, Confident, Conflicted, Congenial, Conscientious, Conservative, Considerate, Conspicuous, Contemptible, Contiguous, Cooperative, Cordial, Courageous, Courteous, Covetous, Creative, Creepy, Critical, Crowded, Crucial, Crude, Cruel, Culpable, Curious, Current, Curt, Cute, Cynical
D	Decent, Deceitful, Decorous, Defensive, Deferential, Deft, Dejected, Delightful, Demeaning, Demise, Dependable, Deplorable, Depressed, Destructive, Devious, Devoted, Dictatorial, Diligent, Diminutive, Diplomatic, Discreet, Disdainful, Dishonest, Dishonorable, Dismal, Disposable, Disrespectful, Distracted, Docile, Downcast, Dynamic
E	Earnest, Earthy, Ecological, Eerie, Efficient, Egotistical, Electrifying, Elitist, Empathetic, Endangered, Endemic, Energetic, Enigmatic, Enthusiastic, Esteemed, Estimable, Ethical, Euphoric, Evergreen, Exclusive, Expectant, Explosive, Exquisite, Extravagant, Extroverted, Exuberant
F	Fabulous, Fair, Faithful, Fallow, False, Famous, Fancy, Ferocious, Fertile, Fervent, Fervid, Fibrous, Fierce, Filthy, Flexible, Focused, Foolish, Forgiving, Forlorn, Fragile, Frailty
G	Generous, Genial, Genteel, Gentle, Genuine, Gifted, Gigantic, Glib, Gloomy, Good, Gorgeous, Gracious, Grand, Grateful, Gravity, Green, Grouchy, Guilty, Gusty
H	Handsome, Happy, Hard-hearted, Healing, Healthy, Heedless, Helpful, Heroic, Homely, Honest, Honorable, Hopeful, Hostile, Humane, Humble, Humorous, Hygienic, Hysterical
I	Idealistic, Idyllic, Ignoble, Ignorant, Ill-tempered, Impartial, Impolite, Improper, Imprudent, Impudent, Indecent, Indecorous, Indifferent, Indigenous, Industrious, Ingenuous, Innocent, Innovative, Insightful, Insolent, Inspirational, Instructive, Insulting, Intense, Intolerant, Introverted, Intuitive, Inventive, Investigative, Irascible, Irresponsible
J	Jaundiced, Jealous, Jocular, Jolly, Jovial, Joyful, Jubilant, Just, Juvenile
K	Keen, Kind, Kindred, Knowledgeable

L	Liberal, Listener, Loathsome, Loving, Loyal
M	Magical, Magnificent, Malevolent, Malicious, Mammoth, Manipulative, Marine, Masterful, Meddling, Meritorious, Meticulous, Migratory, Mindful, Minuscule, Miserable, Mistrustful, Modest, Moral, Muddy, Mushy, Mysterious
N	Naive, Nascent, Native, Natural, Nature, Needy, Nefarious, Negative, Neglected, Neglectful, Negligent, Nice, Noble, Notorious
O	Obedient, Observant, Open, Open-minded, Opinionated, Oppressive, Orderly, Oriented, Original, Outrageous, Outspoken
P	Parasitic, Partial, Passionate, Patient, Perceptive, Personable, Personal, Petulant, Pleasant, Poised, Polite, Polluted, Popular, Powerful, Prejudicial, Preposterous, Pretentious, Prideful, Principled, Pristine, Prompt, Proper, Punctual, Purposeful
Q	Quaint, Quarrelsome, Quick, Quiet, Quirky
R	Radioactive, Rancorous, Rash, Rational, Reasonable, Reckless, Refined, Reflective, Reliant, Relevant, Remarkable, Remorseful, Renewable, Reproductive, Repugnant, Resilient, Resolute, Resourceful, Respectful, Responsible, Responsive, Restorative, Reverent, Rotting, Rude, Ruthless
S	Sad, Safe, Scornful, Scrumptious, Selfish, Sensible, Sensitive, Sharing, Shy, Simple, Sober, Solar, Solemn, Solitary, Soluble, Sour, Spatial, Special, Splendid, Spotless, Staunch, Stern, Stormy, Stunning, Stupendous, Successful, Sullen, Superb, Superior, Supportive, Surly, Suspicious, Sweet, Sweltering, Swollen, Sympathetic
T	Tactful, Tainted, Temperate, Tenacious, Terrific, Testy, Thoughtful, Thoughtless, Tolerant, Towering, Toxic, Treacherous, Trite, Tropical, Trustworthy, Truthful
U	Ultimate, Uncivil, Uncouth, Undeveloped, Underdeveloped, Unethical, Unfair, Uninterested, Unique, United, Unified, Unmannerly, Unrefined, Unsavory, Unsightly, Unworthy, Uplifting, Upright, Uprooted, Upset, Upstanding, Uptight
V	Vast, Valiant, Veracious, Versatile, Vicious, Victorious, Vigilant, Vigorous, Vile, Villainous, Virtuous, Visible, Vivacious, Vocal, Volatile, Volunteering, Vulnerable
W	Wandering, Warm, Wary, Waspish, Watchful, Weary, Welcoming, Wicked, Wide-eyed, Wild, Willing, Winning, Winsome, Wise, Wishy-washy, Wistful, Witty, Woeful, Wonderful, Worldwide, Worrier, Worrisome, Worthwhile, Worthy, Wretch, Wrong
Y	Yappy, Yawning, Yearning, Yellow, Yielding, Yourself, Youthful, Yucky, Yummy
Z	Zany, Zealot, Zealous, Zen, Zero-tolerant, Zesty, Zigzag, Zingy, Zippy, Zonked

Superstitions

Common Superstitions
- Knock on wood—reverse bad luck or avoid "tempting the fates"
- "Bless you"—expelling an evil spirit
- Ears are burning—being talked about
- Itchy palms—a greedy person

Numbers
- Bad luck comes in 3s
- 8—represents balance & harmony
- 666—the mark of the devil
- 13—triskaidekaphobia is the fear of this number hotels skip this floor because this fear is common
- 4—in the Far East 4 is like 13 in the West

Signs of Good Luck
- Cross your fingers for luck
- Finding a four-leaf clover
- Beginner's luck
- Wish on a star
- Lucky penny
- Lucky Dice
- Wishbone
- Horseshoes
- Rabbit's foot

Signs of Bad Luck
- Opening an umbrella indoors
- Walking under a ladder
- Shoes on a table
- Spilling salt
- Hat on a bed
- Breaking a mirror
- Stepping on a crack
- A black cat crossing your path—a witch companion who can turn into a witch after being a cat for 7 years

Bad Omens
- Friday the 13th—the day of bad luck
- Dogs howling—death omen
- Owl hooting—someone you know will die
- Wild bird in your home—death omen
- Black butterfly—a sign of death
- Blood moon—a sign of war
- Gazing at the full moon too long will bring out the lunatic from deep inside you

CHARACTER MOTIVATIONS

In order to have a well-rounded character, they should have multiple reasons that motivate them to do the things they do. No character is purely good or evil, but a mixture of both.

Reasons for Characters to Act			
Acceptance	Disgust	Justice	Rage
Adventure	Duty	Knowledge	Rebellion
Alienation	Eagerness	Legacy	Reconciliation
Ambition	Empathy	Loneliness	Redemption
Anxiety	Envy	Loss	Regret
Avoidance	Escape	Love	Religion
Career	Failure	Lust	Resentment
Catastrophe	Fame	Money	Resolution
Codependence	Fear	Morality	Revenge
Comfort	Friends	Outrage	Rivalry
Compassion	Frustration	Peer Pressure	Satisfaction
Contempt	Glory	Perfectionism	Self-Improvement
Contentment	Greed	Persecution	Shame
Control	Grief	Pity	Sickness
Corruption	Guilt	Pleasure	Stubbornness
Credit	Hate	Popularity	Survival
Curiosity	Honor	Power	Thrills
Cursed	Horror	Prejudice	Torment
Debt	Hurt	Prestige	Valor
Desperation	Ideology	Pride	Vengeance
Destiny	Infatuation	Protection	War
Discovery	Insanity	PTSD	Wrath
Other:			

COMMON HORROR TROPES

DO THE OPPOSITE OR INNOVATE

Use these clichés to your advantage

- Tripping for No Reason
- Couple Who Wanders Off
- No Phone Signal
- Jack-in-the-Box Evil Cat
- Creepy, Unearthly Kids
- Let's Split Up
- Mirror Reflection Jump Scare
- Vehicle Break Down
- Old Crone's Warning
- What's That Sound?
- Where Are the Adults?
- Hide-And-Seek
- Indestructible Killer
- Useless Authority Figure
- Based on a "True Story"
- Just a Dream Fakeout
- Foot in a Bear Trap
- Buried Alive
- Fumbling for the Right Key
- Ghost Story Becomes Real
- It Was There The Whole Time
- I Can See You
- Not a Mask
- It Won't Turn Off
- Homicidal Machine
- Ghostly Chill
- Everything Is Trying to Kill You
- Moving Eyes in the Portrait
- Rescue Fakeout--Rescuer Killed
- Evil Dolls
- Backwoods Creepers
- Evil Hitchhiker
- Supernatural Beings
- Mental Asylums
- Psycho Killer
- Evil Clowns
- Haunted House
- Ghosts
- Poltergeists
- Someone Died Here
- On a Burial Ground
- Afraid of the Dark
- Killer in the Backseat
- Something in the Basement
- Infected by Evil
- Fakeout Escape
- We Can't Leave
- Picked Off One-by-One
- Let's Investigate
- Nowhere to Hide
- Abandoned Place
- Vengeful Spirit
- Running Upstairs Instead of Outside
- Death Scene Jump Scare Take Two

WORDS FOR SOUNDS

Add appeal to your writing by making a splash with descriptive sound words.

Ahem	Clatter	Grind	Pound	Splash	Tweet
Baa	Click	Groan	Pow	Splat	Vroom
Babble	Clink	Gulp	Pulsing	Splinter	Wail
Bang	Clomp	Gurgle	Purr	Sputter	Wallop
Bark	Clonk	Guzzle	Quack	Squawk	Whack
Beat	Clop	Hammer	Racket	Squeak	Wheeze
Beep	Cluck	Hiss	Rap	Squish	Whicker
Bellow	Clunk	Hoot	Ratchet	Stomp	Whinny
Blare	Crackle	Howl	Rattle	Suck	Whip
Blast	Crash	Hubbub	Revved	Swish	Whir
Bleep	Creak	Hum	Ring	Swoop	Whisper
Blip	Crinkle	Jangle	Rip	Swoosh	Whistle
Blow	Crunch	Jingle	Roar	Tap	Whiz
Boing	Din	Kerplunk	Rumble	Tatter	Woof
Bong	Ding	Knock	Rushing	Tee-Hee	Woot
Boo	Discord	Lash	Rustle	Throb	Yap
Boom	Drip	Mew	Scream	Thud	Yawp
Bop	Drone	Mewl	Screech	Thump	Yelp
Bray	Drum	Murmur	Scuff	Thunder	Yip
Bubble	Eek	Neigh	Shriek	Thwack	Yowl
Burp	Fanfare	Oink	Shuffle	Tick	Zap
Buzz	Fizz	Ooze	Sizzle	Tinkle	Zip
Cacophony	Fizzle	Patter	Slam	Titter	Zoom
Cha-Ching	Flick	Peal	Slap	Tock	
Cheep	Fling	Peep	Slop	Tolling	Other:
Chime	Flop	Pew	Slurp	Toot	
Chirp	Fracas	Pitter-Patter	Smack	Trill	
Chug	Giggle	Plink	Snap	Tromp	
Clack	Glug	Plod	Snicker	Trumpet	
Clamor	Glurp	Plop	Snigger	Tsk	
Clang	Gnashing	Plunk	Snip	Tumult	
Clank	Gobble	Poof	Snort	Tut	
Clap	Grating	Pop	Spatter	Twang	

CHARACTER NAMES

Here is a sampling of popular names from all over the world. Have fun mixing and matching.

Female	Unisex	Male	Last	Last
Emma	Jordan	Aiden	Chapman	Holland
Ming	Evan	Joseph	Gonzalez	Church
Anya	Rani	Simon	Bray	Alexander
Eden	Taylor	Martin	Willis	Henry
Hazel	Avril	Juan	Nguyen	Meyer
Julia	Dakota	Tobias	Fitzgerald	Schmidt
Sarah	Rene	Adam	Thompson	Khan
Priya	Desta	Omar	Lee	Wu
Veronica	Bailey	Luka	Hernandez	Takada
Scarlet	Kai	Peter	Fowler	Blevins
Molly	Morgan	Julian	Bauer	Short
Mina	Ashton	David	Dawson	Long
Jing	Justice	Noah	Weber	Katz
Katya	Nash	Logan	Frost	Osborne
Aimee	Courtney	Ivan	Lang	Torres
Fatima	Jo	Liam	Shields	Wolf
Sofia	Genesis	Hugo	Garcia	Mays
Maria	Eko	Emir	Binder	Sanders
Aya	Blue	Arthur	O'Conner	Segal
Mariam	Nyx	Diego	Yu	Jacobs
Hana	Jun	Arjun	Klein	Hancock
Ella	Hayden	Bernardo	Hadad	Lambert
Jada	Dana	Jonathan	Watanabe	Rodriguez
Katarina	Teagan	Reza	Lawrence	Mortensen

CHARACTER APPEARANCE CHARTS

Eye Color	Blue	Sky Blue	Baby Blue	Electric Blue	Cornflower
	Brown	Chestnut	Chocolate	Cognac	Amber
	Green	Sea Green	Moss Green	Jade	Emerald
	Grey	Silver	Gunmetal Grey	Charcoal	Black
	Hazel	Russet	Nut	Honey	Yellow
	Lavender	Other:			
Eye Shape	Almond	Round	Drooping	Hooded	Close-Set
	Wide-Set	Deep-Set	Protruding	Sleepy	Squinting
	Down-Turned	Other:			
Skin Tone	Fair	Ivory	Porcelain	Milky	Snow
	Ruddy	Rose	Peach	Ochre	Golden
	Olive	Khaki	Toffee	Honey	Tawny
	Dark	Ebony	Sepia	Russet	Mahogany
	Other:				
Body Shape	Triangle	Rectangle	Hourglass	Rounded	Diamond
	Inverted Triangle	Barrel	Willowy	Husky	Wiry
	Other:				
Facial Shapes	Oval	Rectangle	Square	Heart	Oblong
	Egg	Diamond	Triangle	Narrow	Block-Like
	Other:				
Hair Color	Black	Dark Brown	Medium Brown	Ash Brown	Golden Brown
	Red	Auburn	Copper	Strawberry	Cinnamon
	Blond	Platinum	White	Silver	Grey
	Other:				

Notes:

HORROR VERSUS THRILLER

Horror and thrillers are often grouped together because they share key elements, but the WAY you deal with your characterization, setting, and point of view will push your story into one camp or the other.

Here are some similarities and differences.

Horror Elements

- Protagonist drives the action
- The protagonist makes a decision to take action in some way
- Goal: to scare the audience
- Most often told in the third person
- We observe the characters
- Often lots of supernatural elements
- Gross-out and shock elements are of high importance
- Extraordinary characters we watch do things

Shared Elements

Fight or Flight
Horrifying
Thrilling
Deadline-Oriented
Something Bad Happened

Thriller Elements

- Antagonist drives the action
- The protagonist unwillingly falls prey to the antagonist's plans
- Goal: to solve a problem
- Most often told in the first person
- We see through the protagonist's eyes and feel what they feel
- Often in a realistic setting
- Anticipation and suspense elements more important
- Ordinary characters we can identify with

CRIME & DETECTIVE VOCABULARY

Are the police involved in your story? Is there a detective unraveling criminal events?

Abduction, Abuse, Access, Accident, Accuse, Action, Admission, Adult, Agency, Aggravated assault, Agree, Alarm, Alert, Alias, Alibi, Allege, APB, Appeal, Appearance, Appraise, Archives, Armed, Arraignment, Arrest, Arson, Ask, Aspect, Assailant, Assault, Assignment, Assistance, Assumptions, Atrocious, Attitude, Attack, Authenticate, Authority, Authorize, Autopsy
Backup, Badge, Badgered, Ballistics, Banned, Basis, Battery, Beaten, Behavior, Belief, Bitter, Blackmail, Blame, Bloodstain, Bodyguard, Bomb squad, Bond, Booking, Branch, Breach, Bribes, Brutal, Brutality, Bullied, Bungled, Burden, Bureau, Burglary, Busted, By-the-book
Capable, Captain, Capture, Careful, Catch, Cautious, Cease, Challenges, Character, Chase, Check out, Citation, Citizen, Civil, Claim, Code, Cold case, Colleague, Collude, Collusion, Commission, Commit, Communication, Community, Competitive, Complaints, Complicated, Concerned, Conduct, Confer, Confess, Confession, Confidential, Confrontation, Consent, Consider, Conspiracy, Conspire, Consult, Contempt, Convict, Conviction, Cooperate, Cop, Coroner, Corrupt, Counterfeit, Court, Crimes, Criminal, Crook, Cruise, Cruel, Culpable
Damage, Danger, Dangerous, Deal, Dealings, Decisions, Dedication, Deduction, Deed, Defense, Deliberate, Delinquent, Deliver, Denial, Deny, Department, Deputy, Detain, Detect, Detective, Determination, Deviant, Dialogue, Difficult, Direct, Disappearance, Discovery, Disobedient, Disorderly, Dispatch, Disregard, Distressing, Disturbing, District attorney, Documentation, Documents, Domestic disputes, Doubtful, Drugs, Drunk, Dupe, Duty, Dying
Eager, Educate, Education, Effect, Embezzle, Emergency, Emphasis, Enable, Encounter, Encumber, Enforce, Entail, Entrap, Equality, Equipment, Espionage, Ethical, Evidence, Examine, Execute, Experience, Expert, Expose, Extort, Extradition, Extreme, Eyes, Expert
Fabricated, Facts, Failure, Fairness, Family, False, Fanatic, Fault, FBI, Federal, Feisty, Felony, Fight, File, Fine, Fingerprint, Fleeting, Flight, Follow, Follow-up, Footprints, Force, Forgery, Formal charges, Foul play, Framed, Fraud, Frantic, Freedom, Full-scale, Fundamental
Gang, Ghastly, Gore, Government, Grief, Guarantee, Guard, Guilty, Gum shoe, Gun
Handcuff, Handle, Harmful, Harass, Hateful, Hazard, Heinous, Helpful, High-powered, Hijack, Hire, Hit man, Holding, Homicide, Honest, Honor, Hooligan, Horrible, Hostage, Hostile
Ill-gotten, Illegal, Illegitimate, Immoral, Imprison, Inappropriate, Incompetent, Imposed, Incapable, Indict, Influence, Informant, Information, Infringe, Initiative, Injury, Innocent, Innuendo, Inquest, Inquire, Instinct, Intelligence, Interests, Interfere, Internet, Interpol, Interpretation, Interstate, Intrude, Intuition, Invade, Investigate, Investigation, Irregular, Issue
Jaded, Jail, Jealous, Joint, Jane Doe, John Doe, Jolt, Judge, Judgment, Judicial, Jury, Justice, Juvenile

Kept out, Kidnapping, Kill, Killer, Kin, Knowledge
Laboratory, Larceny, Law, Lawful, Lawless, Lawsuit, Lease, Legacy, Legal, Legitimate, Liable, Libel, Liberty, Licensed, Lie, Lieutenant, Limit, Line up, Links, Long hours, Lurk
Mace, Magistrate, Maintain, Majority, Malevolence, Malice, Malicious, Manacled, Manner, Manslaughter, Mayhem, Menace, Minority, Miscreant, Misdemeanor, Missing person, Mission, Mob, Motivation, Motive, Motor pool, Motorist, Murder, Mystery
National, Negligence, Negotiate, Neighborhood, Notation, Notification, Nuisance
Oath, Obey, Obligation, Obscure, Obsession, Odd, Offender, Offense, Officer, Official, Omission, On-going, Open case, Opinion, Opportunity, Order, Organize, Ownership
Paper work, Parole, Partner, Partnership, Patrol, Patterns, Payback, Pedestrian, Penalize, Penalty, Penitentiary, Penny-ante, Peril, Perjury, Perpetrator, Phony, Plain-clothes officer, Plead, Police, Police academy, Power, Precedent, Prevention, Previous, Principle, Priors, Prison, Private, Probable cause, Probation officer, Procedure, Process, Professional, Profile, Proof, Property, Prosecutor, Protection, Prove, Provision, Public, Punishment
Qualification, Quality, Quantify, Quantity, Quarrel, Quell, Query, Question, Quick, Quirks
Radar, Rank, Reading rights, Reasons, Record, Recruit, Red-handed, Redemption, Redress, Reduction, Refute, Register, Registration, Regulation, Reinforcements, Reject, Release, Report, Reports, Reprobate, Reputation, Research, Resist, Response, Responsibility, Restraining order, Restrict, Retainer, Revenge, Rights, Riot, Robbery, Rogue, Routine, Rules
Sabotage, Safeguard, Safety, Sanction, Scandal, Scene, Scum bag, Sealed record, Search and rescue team, Searching, Secret, Seize, Select, Sentence, Sergeant, Seriousness, Serve, Services, Sheriff, Shift, Shooting, Shyster, Sighting, Situation, Skilled, Slander, Slaying, Sleazy, Sleuthing, Smuggling, Snitch, Solution, Solve, Sources, Squad, Stalk, State, Statute, Statute of limitation, Stipulation, Strangulation, Study, Subdue, Subpoena, Successful, Sully, Summons, Suppression, Surveillance, Suspect, Suspected, Suspicion, Suspicious, Sworn, System
Tactics, Tantamount, Taping, Task force, Taser, Technique, Tense, Tension, Testify, Testimony, Theory, Threat, Threatening, Thwart, Tip, Torture, Trace, Traffic, Tragedy, Transfer, Trap, Trauma, Traumatize, Treatment, Trespass, Trial, Trooper, Trust, Truth
Unacceptable, Unauthorized, Unclaimed, Unconstitutional, Undercover, Underpaid, Unintentional, Unit, Unjust, Unknown, Unlawful, Uphold, Urgency, Utilize
Vagrant, Vandalism, Vanish, Venomous, Verdict, Verification, Victim, Victimize, Vicious, Viewpoint, Vigilante, Villain, Violate, Violation, Violence, Volume, Vow
Wanted, Wanton, Ward, Warped, Warrant, Watch, Weapon, Weird, Whodunit, Wicked, Wild, Will, Wiretap, Wisdom, Witness, Worried, Wrong, Wrongdoing

Yappy, Yell, Yonder, Young, Youth	Zap, Zeal, Zealous, Zest, Zero, Zilch, Zippy

SYNONYMS

As you are editing, it is important to pay attention to repetition. Much of the tinkering with words will come with editing, but I love using synonym sheets to cut down on the editing later, as well as to inspire me.

Emotions

Other words for **Happy**

Alluring, amused, appealing, appeased, blissful, blithe, carefree, charmed, cheeky, chipper, chirpy, content, convivial, delighted, elated, electrified, ecstatic, enchanted, enthusiastic, exultant, excited, fantastic, fulfilled, glad, gleeful, glowing, gratified, idyllic, intoxicating, jolly, joyful, joyous, jovial, jubilant, light, lively, merry, mirthful, overjoyed, pleased, pleasant, radiant, sparkling, savoured, satisfied, serene, sunny, thrilled, tickled, up, upbeat, winsome, wonderful.

Other words for **SAD**

Aching, agitated, anguished, anxious, bleak, bothered, brooding, bugged, chagrined, cheerless, darkly, disillusioned, disappointed, disenchanted, disheartened, dismayed, distraught, dissatisfied, despondent, doleful, failed, faint, frustrated, glazed, gloomy, glowering, haunted, hopeless, languid, miserable, pained, perturbed, sour, suffering, sullen, thwarted, tormented, troubled, uneasy, unsettled, upset, vacant, vexed, wan, woeful, wounded.

Other words for **Mad**

Affronted, aggravated, agitated, angered, annoyed, bitter, boiling, bothered, brooding, bugged, bummed, cantankerous, chafed, chagrined, crabby, cross, disgruntled, distraught, disturbed, enflamed, enraged, exasperated, fiery, fuming, furious, frantic, galled, goaded, hacked, heated, hostile, hot, huffy, ill-tempered, incensed, indignant, inflamed, infuriated, irate, ireful, irritated, livid, maddened, malcontent, miffed, nettled, offended, peeved, piqued, provoked, raging, resentful, riled, scowling, sore, sour, stung, taut, tense, tight, troubled, upset, vexed, wrathful.

Other words for **Crying**

Bawling, blubbering, gushing, howling, lamenting, moaning, scream-crying, silent tears, sniffling, snivelling, sobbing, sorrowing, teary, wailing, weepy, woeful.

Commonly Used Words

Other words for ASKED

Appealed, begged, beckoned, beseeched, besieged, bid, craved, commanded, claimed, coaxed, challenged, charged, charmed, cross-examined, demanded, drilled, entreated, enchanted, grilled, implored, imposed, interrogated, invited, invoked, inquired, insisted, needled, ordered, pleaded, petitioned, picked, probed, pried, pressed, pumped, pursued, put through the wringer, put the screws down, questioned, queried, quizzed, requested, required, requisitioned, roasted, solicited, summoned, surveyed, sweated, urged, wanted, wheedled, wooed, worried, wondered.

Other words for LAUGH

Break up, burst, cackle, chortle, chuckle, crack-up, crow, giggle, grin, guffaw, hee-haw, howl, peal, quack, roar, scream, shriek, snicker, snigger, snort, split one's sides, tee-hee, titter, whoop.

Other Words for LOOK

Address, admire, attention, audit, babysit, beam, beholding, blink, bore, browse, burn, cast, check, comb, consider, contemplate, delve, detect, discover, disregard, distinguish, ensure, evil eye, examine, explore, eye, eyeball, ferret, fix, flash, forage, gander, gaze, get an eyeful, give the eye, glance, glare, glaze, glimmer, glimpse, glitter, gloat, goggle, grope, gun, have a gander, inquire, inspect, investigate, judge, keeping watch, leaf-through, leer, lock daggers on, look fixedly, look-see, marking, moon, mope, neglect, note, notice, noting, observe, ogle, once-over, peek, peep, peer, peg, peruse, poke into, scan, pout, probe, pry, quest, rake, recognize, reconnaissance, regard, regarding, renew, resemble, review, riffle, rubberneck, rummage, scan, scowl, scrutinize, search, seeing, sense, settle, shine, sift, simper, size-up, skim, slant, smile, smirk, snatch, sneer, speculative, spot, spy, squint, stare, study, sulk, supervise, surveillance, survey, sweep, take stock of, take in, trace, verify, view, viewing, watch, witness, yawp, zero in.

Other words for REPLIED

Acknowledged, answered, argued, accounted, barked, bit, be in touch, boomeranged, comeback, countered, conferred, claimed, denied, echoed, feedback, fielded the question, get back to, growled, matched, parried, reacted, reciprocated, rejoined, responded, retorted, remarked, returned, retaliated, shot back, snapped, squelched, squared, swung, vacillated.

Other words for **Sat**
Be seated, bear on, cover, ensconce, give feet a rest, grab a chair, have a place, have a seat, hunker, install, lie, park, perch, plop down, pose, posture, put it there, relax, remain, rest, seat, seat oneself, settle, squat, take a load off, take a place, take a seat.

Other words for **Was/Were**   VERB (TO BE)
Abided, acted, be alive, befell, breathed, continued, coexisted, do, endured, ensued, existed, had been, happened, inhabited, lasted, lived, moved, obtained, occurred, persisted, prevailed, remained, rested, stood, stayed, survived, subsided, subsisted, transpired.

Other words for **Walk**
Advance, amble, barge, bolt, bounce, bound, canter, charge, crawl, creep, dance, dash, escort, gallop, hike, hobble, hop, jog, jump, leap, limp, lope, lumber, meander, mosey, move, pad, pace march, parade, patrol, plod, prance, proceed, promenade, prowl, race, roam, rove, run, sashay, saunter, scamper, scramble, zip shuffle, skip, slink, slither, slog, sprint, stagger, step, stomp, stride, stroll, strut, stumble, swagger, thread, tiptoe, traipse, tramp, tread, trek, trip, trot, trudge, wade, wander.

Other words for **Whisper**
Breathed, buzz, disclosed, exhaled, expressed, fluttered, gasped, hint, hiss, hum, hushed tone, intoned, lament, low voice, moaned, mouthed, mumble, murmur, mutter, puff, purred, reflected, ruffle, rumble, rush, said low, said softly, sigh, sob, undertone, utter, voiced, wheezed.

Other words for **Went**
Abscond, ambled, approached, avoided, be off, beat it, bolted, bounced, bounded, bugged out, burst, carved, cleared out, crawled, crept, cruised, cut and run, danced, darted, dashed, decamped, deserted, disappeared, ducked out, escaped, evaded, exited, fared, fled, floated, flew, flew the coop, galloped, got away, got going, got lost, glided, go down, go south, hightailed, hit the road, hoofed it, hopped, hotfooted, hurdled, hustled, journeyed, jumped, leapt, left, lighted out, loped, lunged, made haste, made a break for it, made for, made off, made tracks, marched, moseyed, moved, muscled, neared, negotiated, paced, paraded, passed, pedalled, proceeded, progressed, pulled out, pulled, pushed off, pushed on, quitted, retired, retreated, rode, ran along, ran away, rushed, sashayed, scampered, scooted, scrammed, scurried, scuttled, set off, set out, shot, shouldered, shoved off, shuffled, skedaddled, skipped out, skipped, skirted, slinked, slipped, soared, split, sprang, sprinted, stole away, steered clear, stepped on it, strolled, strutted, scurried, swept, took a hike, took a powder, took flight, took leave, took off, threaded, toddled, tottered, trampled, travelled, traversed, trekked, trode, trudged, tumbled, vamoosed, vanished, vaulted, veered, walked off, wandered, weaved, wended, whisked, withdrew, wormed, zipped, zoomed.

Other words for SAID

Accused, acknowledged, added, announced, addressed, admitted, advised, affirmed, agreed, asked, avowed, asserted, answered, apologized, argued, assured, approved, articulated, alleged, attested, barked, bet, bellowed, babbled, begged, bragged, began, bawled, bleated, blurted, boomed, broke in, bugged, boasted, bubbled, beamed, burst out, believed, brought out, confided, crowed, coughed, cried, congratulated, complained, conceded, chorused, concluded, confessed, chatted, convinced, chattered, cheered, chided, chimed in, clucked, coaxed, commanded, cautioned, continued, commented, called, croaked, chuckled, claimed, choked, chortled, corrected, communicated, claimed, contended, criticized, construe,

dared, decided, disagreed, described, disclosed, drawled, denied, declared, demanded, divulged, doubted, denied, disputed, dictated, echoed, ended, exclaimed, explained, expressed, enunciated, expounded, emphasized, formulated, fretted, finished, gulped, gurgled, gasped, grumbled, groaned, guessed, gibed, giggled, greeted, growled, grunted, hinted, hissed, hollered, hypothesized, inquired, imitated, implied, insisted, interjected, interrupted, intoned, informed, interpreted, illustrated, insinuated, jeered, jested, joked, justified, lied, laughed, lisped, maintained, muttered, marveled, moaned, mimicked, mumble, modulated, murmured, mused, mentioned, mouthed, nagged, noted, nodded, noticed,

objected, observed, offered, ordered, owned up, piped, pointed out, panted, pondered, praised, prayed, puzzled, proclaimed, promised, proposed, protested, purred, pled, pleaded, put in, prevailed, parried, pressed, put forward, pronounced, pointed out, prescribed, popped off, persisted, protested, questioned, quavered, quipped, quoted, queried, rejected, reasoned, ranted, reassured, reminded, responded, recalled, returned, requested, roared, related, remarked, replied, reported, revealed, rebutted, retorted, repeated, reckoned, remembered, regarded, recited, resolved, reflected, ripped, rectified, reaffirmed,

snickered, sniffed, smirked, snapped, snarled, shot, sneered, sneezed, started, stated, stormed, sobbed, stuttered, suggested, surmised, sassed, sputtered, sniffled, snorted, spoke, stammered, squeaked, sassed, scoffed, scolded, screamed, shouted, sighed, smiled, sang, shrieked, shrilled, speculated, supposed, settled, solved, shot back, swore, stressed, spilled, told, tested, trilled, taunted, teased, tempted, theorized, threatened, tore, uttered, unveiled, urged, upheld, vocalized, voiced, vindicated, volunteered, vowed, vented, verbalized, warned, wailed, went on, wept, whimpered, whined, wondered, whispered, worried, warranted, yawned, yakked.

MY SYNONYM LISTS:

OTHER NOTES & RESEARCH

BOOKS BY ROBIN WOODS

Award-Winning Novels

Fairy Tale Retelling

Beauty & the Beast
+
Role Swap
+
Vikings
=
"Absolute Magic"

Young Adult Urban Fantasy

For ultimate suspense, read the prequel after book two.

The Watcher Series

Extras can be read along with the books.

Allure | The Unintended | The Nexus | The Sacrifice | The Fallen Part 1 | The Fallen Part 2 | Light & Shadow

Award-Winning Creative Writing Series

General Writing Inspiration for All Ages

For Kids (and Kids at Heart)

Large Project

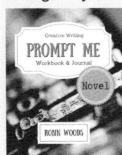

Perfect for a "Book Bible" for each of your working projects.

Keep organized with charts and graphic organizers.

Genre Specific Inspiration

Digital   **Reading Log**

Mystery & Suspense
Sci-Fi & Fantasy
Romance
Horror & Thriller

Gratitude & Self-Care
Coming Soon

Dive into a genre and empower your creativity.

Prompt Me Sci-Fi & Fantasy

All new photos and prompts

New activities

Prompt Me Romance

More master lists

More inspiration

Picture This: Photo Prompts & Inspiration

Meet *Prompt Me's* Digital Cousin
52 Full Color Photo Prompts
92 Written Prompts with 422 combinations
14 Master Lists
Tip, Tricks, and Challenges

Great for writers on the go!

ABOUT THE AUTHOR

Robin Woods is a former high school and university instructor with two and a half decades of experience teaching English, literature, and writing. She has earned a BA in English and an MA in Education.

In addition to teaching, Robin Woods has published six highly-rated novels and has multiple projects in the works.

For a free book and access to her Writer's Tool Kit, join her mailing list. She promises not to fill your inbox.

FREE BOOK *plus* THE WRITER'S TOOL KIT

Free when you join the mailing list.

ww.RobinWoodsFiction.com

Thank you for reading. If you enjoyed this book, please take a moment to write a review. It is the best way to help the authors you love. Books without reviews simply don't sell and your support is critical. Reviews don't have to be long. Something as simple as:
I liked ___ and ___. I would recommend it to ___.   Thank you so much. Blessings!